Handwriting

practice made fun

focus on size & placement

Growing Minds
PRESS

Visit Us Online

Download Free Printables

growingmindspress.wixsite.com/home

Follow us on social media:

Please remember to leave us a review.

SCAN ME

Our Print Handwriting Program

Our print handwriting program is a comprehensive series of five books that includes instructional workbooks with corresponding animated YouTube videos, practice workbooks, and free resources on our website. We use a systematic approach that is outlined on the next few pages.

Book #1: Pre-writing Practice Made Fun: Preschool Writing Activities
Grades: Preschool – Pre-Kindergarten (ages 3-5)

Pre-writing and Fine Motor Skills

With this workbook, preschoolers can practice pre-writing strokes in preparation for letter and number formation. We have intentionally omitted lowercase letters in order to maintain a developmentally appropriate focus on pre-writing strokes, uppercase letters, and numbers. As developing fine motor skills is critical for handwriting success, we provide free resources on our website to assist you in fostering this important area of your child's development. We recommend using small golf size pencils or crayons broken in half to help your preschooler with their grasp while they enjoy this workbook.

Book #2: Handwriting Practice Made Fun: Focus on Formation
Grades: Pre-Kindergarten – 1st Grade (ages 4-7)

A Solid Foundation in Handwriting

Learning letter and number formation is a critical component for a solid foundation in handwriting. This workbook provides important step-by-step instruction presented in a stroke-based teaching order built on developmental progression. We focus on correct handwriting formation so that learners can eventually write letters and numbers with automaticity. We also encourage you to continue using the free and fun fine motor activities on our website for a positive impact on your child's handwriting development.

Our Print Handwriting Program

Animated Lesson Videos

A unique and valuable part of our program is our free animated lesson videos featuring our lovable joke-telling character, Funny Bunny Frankie. These videos bring handwriting to life by demonstrating how each letter and number is formed using simple movements that your child can easily understand. Together, this workbook and the corresponding videos provide a multi-sensory approach that will appeal to all learners.

Letter Reversals or Dyslexia?

We also address the common problem of letter reversals. Many parents believe when they see their child writing letters backwards or upside down that it is indicative of dyslexia. This is a misconception. It is normal for children under the age of 8 to write letters in reverse. With our program, we address letter reversals early, which can prevent the issue from starting or continuing. If your child is age 8 or older and continues to write letters in reverse after specifically addressing letter reversals, then we recommend consulting a professional as it may or may not be related to dyslexia.

Book #3: Handwriting Practice Made Fun: Focus on Size and Placement
Grades: 1st Grade – 3rd Grade (ages 6-9)

Handwriting Size and Placement

The next step in our handwriting program teaches your child how to correctly size and place letters and numbers on handwriting lines. Being aware of how to effectively use the handwriting lines will help your learner improve their handwriting skills. We continue our stroke-based teaching order to reinforce handwriting formation while they build the next progression of skills.

Our Print Handwriting Program

Animated Videos

Our lovable joke-telling friend Funny Bunny Frankie is back in this workbook and in animated videos to introduce his friends the Alpha Buddies. Together they will show your learner how to identify where each letter and number belong on the handwriting lines. These fun videos teach your child the purpose of each line and will keep them engaged while they focus on the size and placement of their handwriting.

Book #4: Handwriting Practice Made Fun: Silly Sentences
Grades: 1st Grade – 4th Grade (ages 6-10)

Letter and Sentence Handwriting Practice

The next workbook in our handwriting series provides letter and sentence practice using sight words. Students will roll a die to select words from lists that will help them build silly sentences. They will copy their silly sentence on handwriting lines and perform self-checks to ensure proper sentence formation. We use a focus letter with each worksheet to provide ample letter practice while also practicing handwriting with sentences. If your child enjoys being silly, they'll enjoy practicing handwriting with this silly and fun workbook.

Book #5: Handwriting Practice Made Fun: Jokes, Riddles, Stories, and More
Grades: 2nd Grade – 4th Grade (ages 7-10)

Sentence Handwriting Practice

This handwriting practice workbook has a variety of fun activities for tracing and copying sentences. Using jokes, riddles, silly stories, fun facts, and decoding learners will practice handwriting in a fun and engaging way. If your child needs any review, they can watch the appropriate videos from our YouTube channel.

Which Book Should I Choose?

We have provided general placement guidelines by grade and age. Consider your child's skill level and needs when making your decision.

Preschool (ages 3-4)

#1: Pre-Writing Practice Made Fun: Preschool Writing Activities

Pre-Kindergarten (ages 4-5)

#1: Pre-Writing Practice Made Fun: Preschool Writing Activities
OR
#2: Handwriting Practice Made Fun: Focus on Formation

If you check one or more of the boxes below, choose Book #1. If not, choose Book #2

❏ My child has had little or no prior pre-writing strokes practice (vertical lines, horizontal lines, circle, cross, diagonal lines, square, X, and triangle)
❏ My child needs more pre-writing stokes practice
❏ My child has difficulty with some of the pre-writing strokes

Which Book Should I Choose?

Kindergarten (ages 5-6)

#2: Handwriting Practice Made Fun: Focus on Formation

1st Grade (ages 6-7)

#2: Handwriting Practice Made Fun: Focus on Formation
OR
#3: Handwriting Practice Made Fun: Focus on Size and Placement
OR
#4: Handwriting Practice Made Fun: Silly Sentences

- ❑ My child needs more help to correctly form letters and numbers (Choose Book #2)
- ❑ My child forms letters and numbers correctly (Choose Book #3)
- ❑ My child has finished Book #3 (Choose Book #4)

Which Book Should I Choose?

2nd Grade – 3rd Grade (ages 7-9)

#3: Handwriting Practice Made Fun: Focus on Size and Placement
OR
#4: Handwriting Practice Made Fun: Silly Sentences
OR
#5: Handwriting Practice Made Fun: Jokes, Riddles, Stories, and More!

- ❏ My child needs help to correctly form some letters or numbers (Choose Book #3)
- ❏ My child needs help to place some letters or numbers correctly on handwriting lines (Choose Book #3)
- ❏ My child needs both letter and sentence handwriting practice (Choose Book #4)
- ❏ My child needs just handwriting practice with sentences (Choose Book #5)

4th Grade (ages 9-10)

#4: Handwriting Practice Made Fun: Silly Sentences
OR
#5: Handwriting Practice Made Fun: Jokes, Riddles, Stories, and More!

- ❏ My child needs both letter and sentence handwriting practice (Choose Book #4)
- ❏ My child needs just handwriting practice with sentences (Choose Book #5)

Watch Our Handwriting Videos

YouTube Channel: Growing Minds Press

To see handwriting in action, watch our free videos on YouTube. The videos for this workbook align perfectly with the content in this workbook. Together, they provide your learner with an interactive learning experience to better understand writing on handwriting lines.

Benefits of This Book

✓ Step-by-step handwriting instruction
✓ Fun teaching style used to engage learners
✓ Stroke based teaching order built on developmental progression
✓ Free videos for learning correct sizing and placement of letters and numbers
✓ Correct letter and number formation with correct directional arrows
✓ Starting positions emphasized for proper handwriting development
✓ Continuous stroke patterns for efficient and fluid handwriting practice
✓ No unnecessary pencil lifting to help avoid awkward stroke order
✓ Reviews to aid with retention of material
✓ Large font size that is developmentally appropriate

Pencil Grip

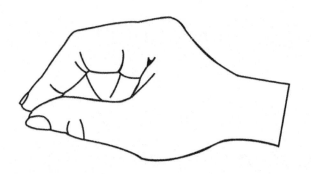

Snappy The Alligator
says "Snap, Snap, Snap!"
Then he picks up his pencil
and makes it flip.
Now, I've got a good grip!

Meet Funny Bunny Frankie

Hi! I'm Funny Bunny Frankie!

Funny Bunny Frankie is not your typical bunny. He loves to write letters and numbers. He's so excited to teach you how to write on handwriting lines! After you are done with this workbook, you'll know how to write your letters and numbers, just like Funny Bunny Frankie!

Let fun learning time begin!

Handwriting Lines

The top line is the tree line.
The middle line is the fence line.
The bottom line is the grass line.
Below the grass is the dirt.

← Tree line

← Fence line

← Grass line
Dirt

Taller letters stand on the grass and are as tall as the trees.

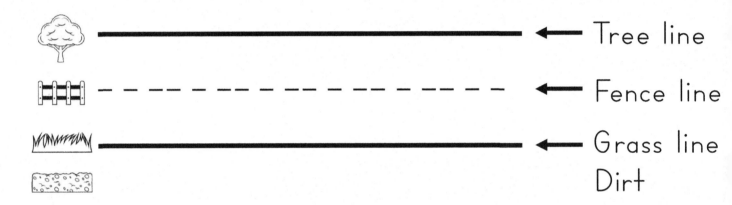

Shorter letters stand on the grass and are as tall as the fence..

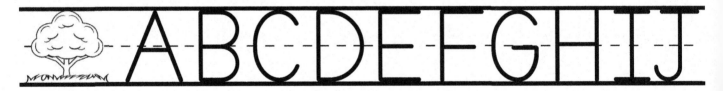

Meet the Alpha Buddies

Meet my friends from Alphaville, the Alpha Buddies!

Tall Letters

Adults

The adults are uppercase letters and they are as tall as the trees in Alphaville.

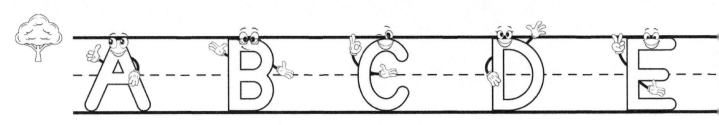

Teenagers

The teenagers are the lowercase letters and are also as tall as the trees.

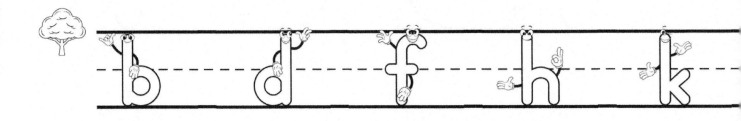

We call the adults and teenagers the TALL letters.

Short Letters

The kids are the lowercase letters that are as tall as the fences in Alphaville.

We call the kids the SHORT letters.

Tail Letters

The pets are lowercase letters that are also as tall as the fences. They dig holes in the ground and then stick their tails in the dirt! Those are some silly pets!

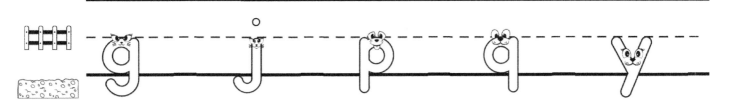

We call the pets the TAIL letters.

This is the letter L on handwriting lines.

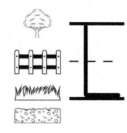

Circle the correct answers below.

L is a	It stands on the	and is as tall as the
tall letter. short letter. tail letter.	tree 🌳 line fence ▦ line grass 🌾 line dirt ▨ line	trees. 🌳 fence. ▦

Start with your pencil on the dot and write the letter.

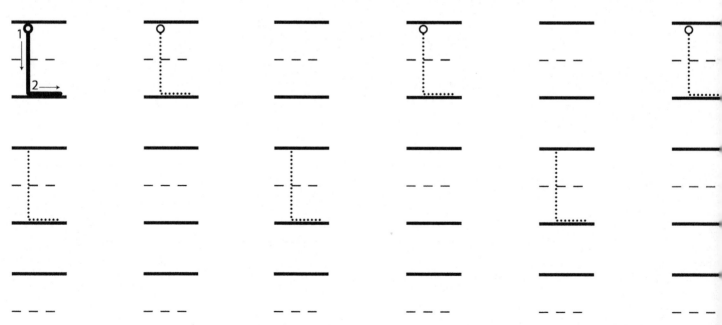

This is the letter F on handwriting lines.

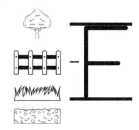

Circle the correct answers below.

F is a	It stands on the	and is as tall as the
tall letter. short letter. tail letter.	tree line fence line grass line dirt line	trees. fence.

Start with your pencil on the dot and write the letter.

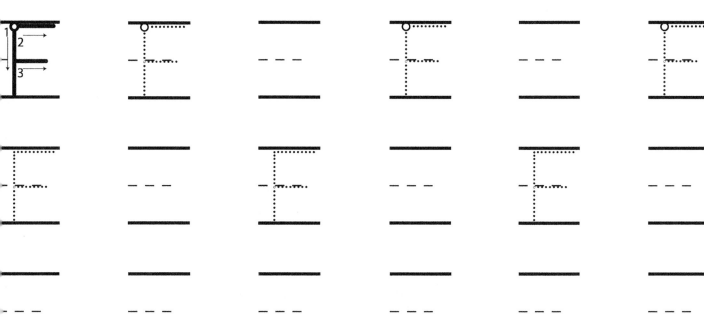

Review

Circle the letters that are in the best positions.

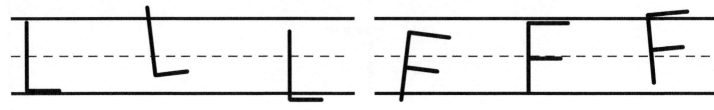

L L L F F F

Trace and copy the letters.

Joke Time!

What do you call a snowman in the summer?

A puddle!

This is the letter E on handwriting lines.

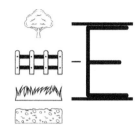

Circle the correct answers below.

E is a	It stands on the	and is as tall as the
tall letter. short letter. tail letter.	tree 🌳 line fence 🚧 line grass 🌾 line dirt 🟫 line	trees. 🌳 fence. 🚧

Start with your pencil on the dot and write the letter.

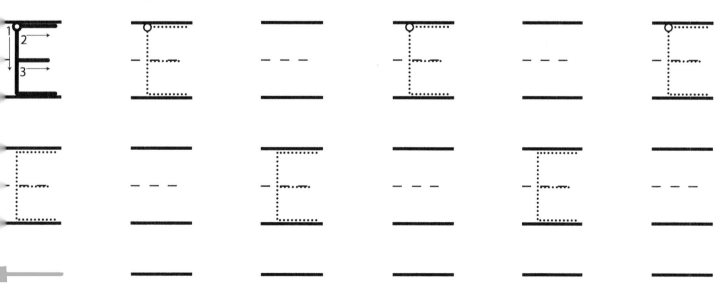

This is the letter H on handwriting lines.

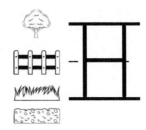

Circle the correct answers below.

H is a	It stands on the	and is as tall as the
tall letter. short letter. tail letter.	tree line fence line grass line dirt line	trees. fence.

Start with your pencil on the dot and write the letter.

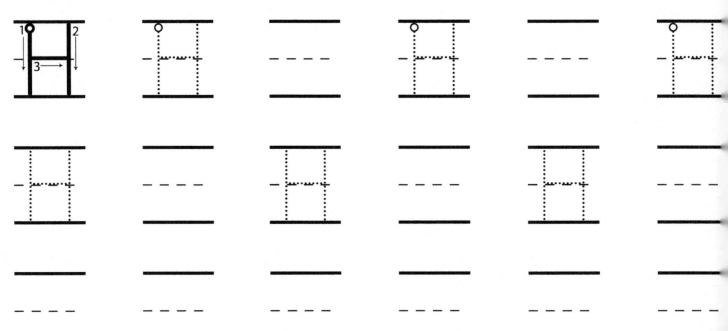

Review

Circle the letters that are in the best positions.

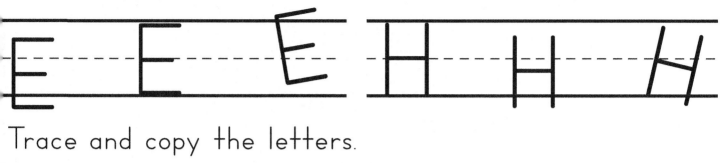

Trace and copy the letters.

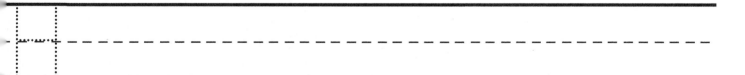

Joke Time!

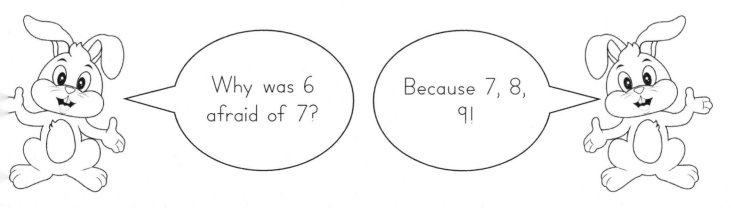

Why was 6 afraid of 7?

Because 7, 8, 9!

This is the letter T on handwriting lines.

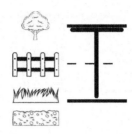

Circle the correct answers below.

T is a	It stands on the	and is as tall as the
tall letter. short letter. tail letter.	tree line fence line grass line dirt line	trees. fence.

Start with your pencil on the dot and write the letter.

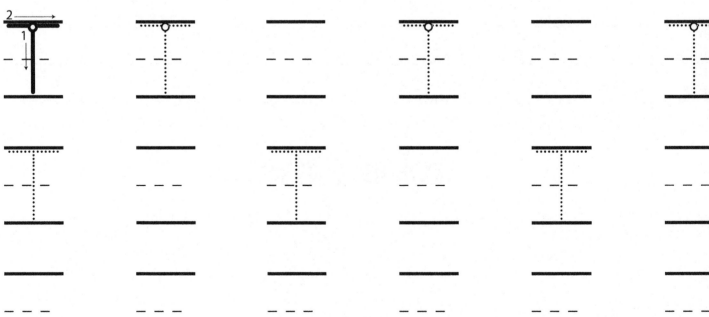

This is the letter I on handwriting lines.

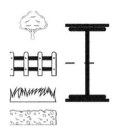

Circle the correct answers below.

I is a	It stands on the	and is as tall as the
tall letter. short letter. tail letter.	tree line fence line grass line dirt line	trees. fence.

Start with your pencil on the dot and write the letter.

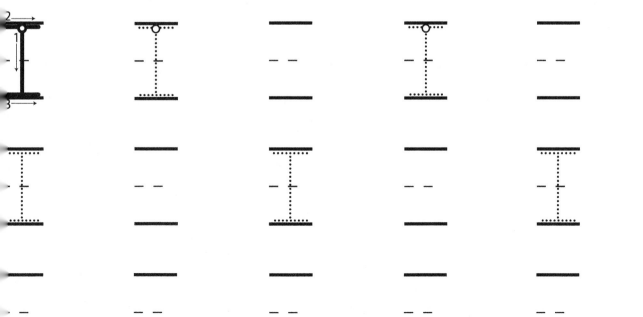

Review

Circle the letters that are in the best positions.

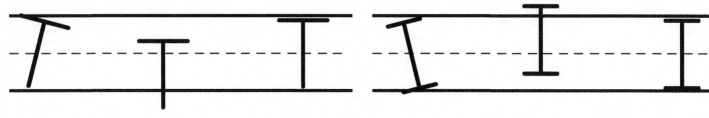

Trace and copy the letters.

Joke Time!

What gets wetter the more it dries?

A towel!

This is the letter D on handwriting lines.

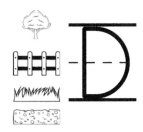

Circle the correct answers below.

D is a	It stands on the	and is as tall as the
tall letter. short letter. tail letter.	tree line fence line grass line dirt line	trees. fence.

Start with your pencil on the dot and write the letter.

This is the letter B on handwriting lines.

Circle the correct answers below.

B is a	It stands on the	and is as tall as the
tall letter. short letter. tail letter.	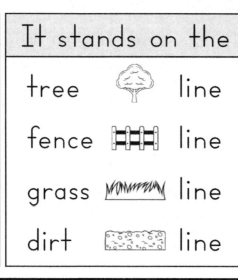 tree line fence line grass line dirt line	 trees. fence.

Start with your pencil on the dot and write the letter.

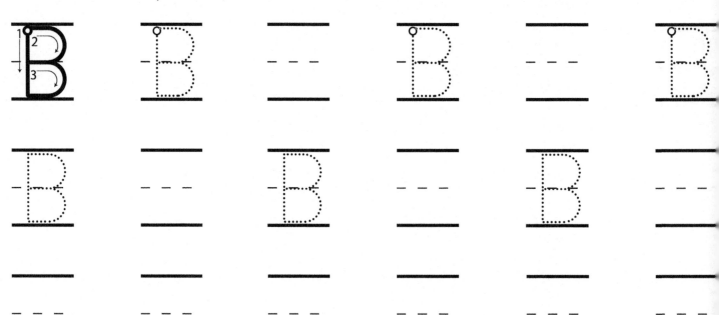

Review

Circle the letters that are in the best positions.

D D D B B B

Trace and copy the letters.

D

D

B

B

Joke Time!

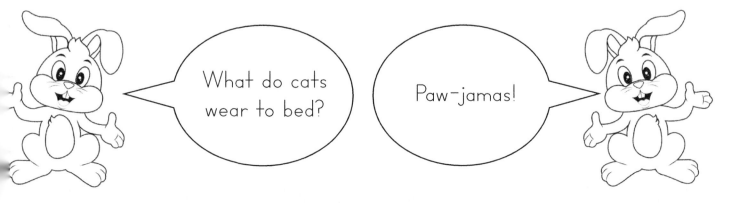

What do cats wear to bed?

Paw-jamas!

Need help forming P? See our YouTube video, How to Write the Uppercase Letter P

This is the letter P on handwriting lines.

Circle the correct answers below.

P is a	It stands on the	and is as tall as the
tall letter.		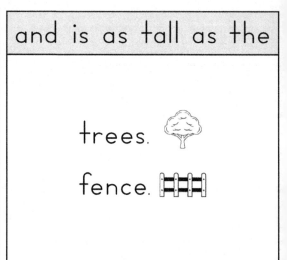
short letter.		
tail letter.		

Start with your pencil on the dot and write the letter.

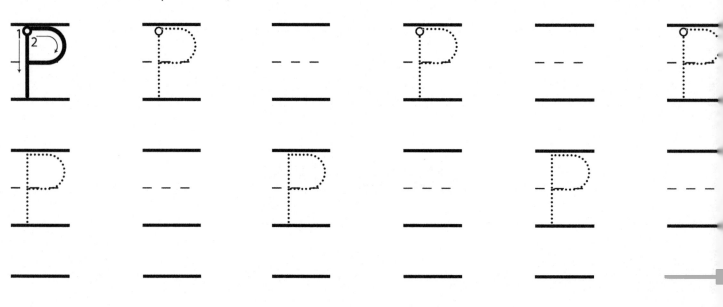

This is the letter J on handwriting lines.

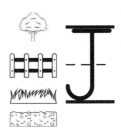

Circle the correct answers below.

J is a	It stands on the	and is as tall as the
tall letter. short letter. tail letter.	tree  line fence  line grass line dirt line	trees. fence. 

Start with your pencil on the dot and write the letter.

Review

Circle the letters that are in the best positions.

P P P J J J

Trace and copy the letters.

P

P

J

J

Joke Time!

What kind of room doesn't have doors?

A mushroom!

This is the letter U on handwriting lines.

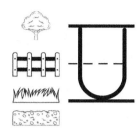

Circle the correct answers below.

U is a	It stands on the	and is as tall as the
tall letter. short letter. tail letter.	tree line fence line grass line dirt line	trees. fence.

Start with your pencil on the dot and write the letter.

This is the letter C on handwriting lines.

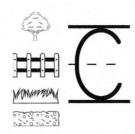

Circle the correct answers below.

C is a	It stands on the	and is as tall as the
tall letter. short letter. tail letter.	tree line fence line grass line dirt line	trees. fence.

Start with your pencil on the dot and write the letter.

Review

Circle the letters that are in the best positions.

U U U C C C

Trace and copy the letters.

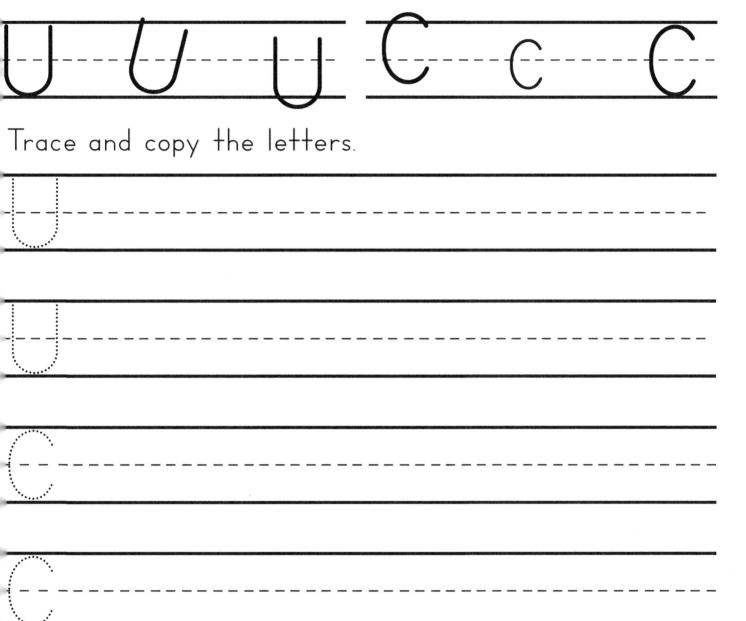

Joke Time!

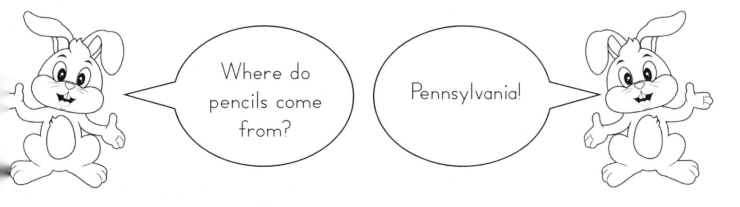

Where do pencils come from?

Pennsylvania!

This is the letter O on handwriting lines.

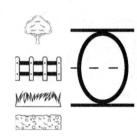

Circle the correct answers below.

O is a	It stands on the	and is as tall as the
tall letter. short letter. tail letter.	tree line fence line grass line dirt line	trees. fence.

Start with your pencil on the dot and write the letter.

This is the letter G on handwriting lines.

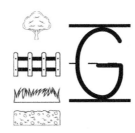

Circle the correct answers below.

G is a	It stands on the	and is as tall as the
tall letter. short letter. tail letter.	tree line fence line grass line dirt line	trees. fence.

Start with your pencil on the dot and write the letter.

Review

Circle the letters that are in the best positions.

O O O G G G

Trace and copy the letters.

O

O

G

G

Joke Time!

What did one tomato say to the other tomato during a race?

Ketchup!

This is the letter Q on handwriting lines.

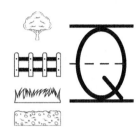

Circle the correct answers below.

Q is a	It stands on the	and is as tall as the
tall letter. short letter. tail letter.	tree line fence line grass line dirt line	trees. fence.

Start with your pencil on the dot and write the letter.

  - - - - - - -

 - - - - - - - - - - - -

This is the letter S on handwriting lines.

Circle the correct answers below.

S is a	It stands on the	and is as tall as the
tall letter. short letter. tail letter.	tree ⬛ line fence ⬛ line grass ⬛ line dirt ⬛ line	trees. ⬛ fence. ⬛

Start with your pencil on the dot and write the letter.

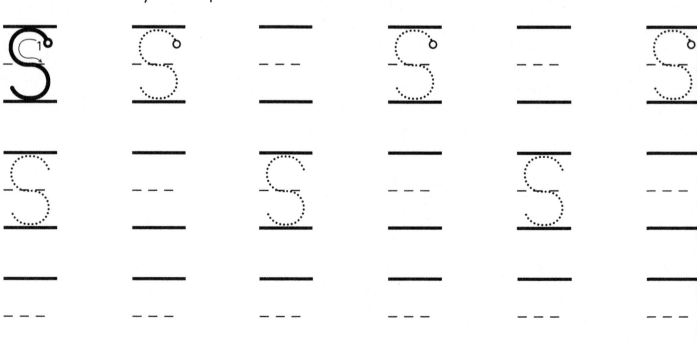

Review

Circle the letters that are in the best positions.

Q   Q   Q   S   S   S

Trace and copy the letters.

Q

Q

S

S

Joke Time!

What did the egg say when it was late for breakfast?

I have to scramble!

This is the letter R on handwriting lines.

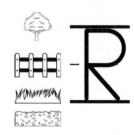

Circle the correct answers below.

R is a	It stands on the	and is as tall as the
tall letter. short letter. tail letter.	tree 🌳 line fence ▦ line grass 〰 line dirt ▨ line	trees. 🌳 fence. ▦

Start with your pencil on the dot and write the letter.

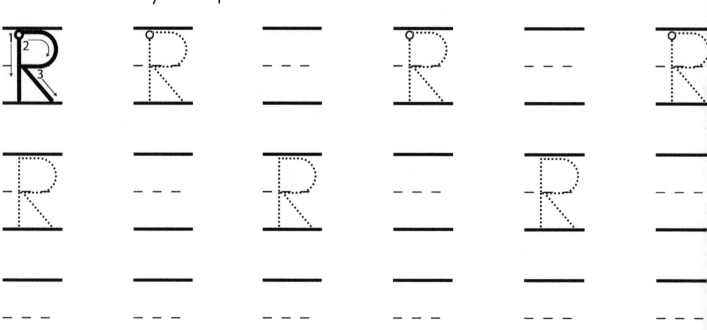

This is the letter A on handwriting lines.

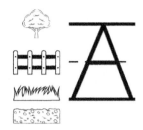

Circle the correct answers below.

A is a	It stands on the	and is as tall as the
tall letter. short letter. tail letter.	tree line fence line grass line dirt line	trees. fence.

Start with your pencil on the dot and write the letter.

Review

Circle the letters that are in the best positions.

R R R A A A A

Trace and copy the letters.

R

R

A

A

Joke Time!

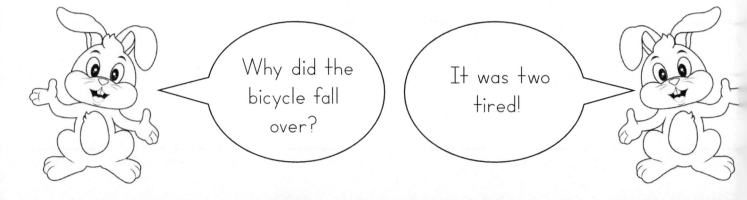

Why did the bicycle fall over?

It was two tired!

This is the letter K on handwriting lines.

Circle the correct answers below.

K is a	It stands on the	and is as tall as the
tall letter. short letter. tail letter.	tree ⬆ line fence ⬆ line grass ⬆ line dirt ⬆ line	trees. ⬆ fence. ⬆

Start with your pencil on the dot and write the letter.

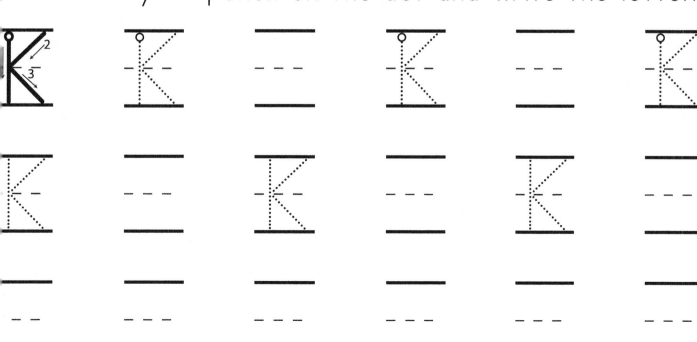

This is the letter M on handwriting lines.

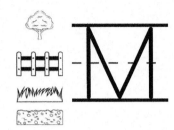

Circle the correct answers below.

M is a	It stands on the	and is as tall as the
tall letter. short letter. tail letter.	tree 🌳 line fence ▦ line grass 〜 line dirt ▭ line	trees. 🌳 fence. ▦

Start with your pencil on the dot and write the letter.

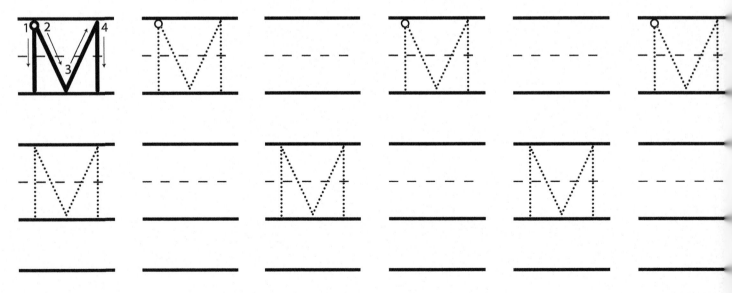

Review

Circle the letters that are in the best positions.

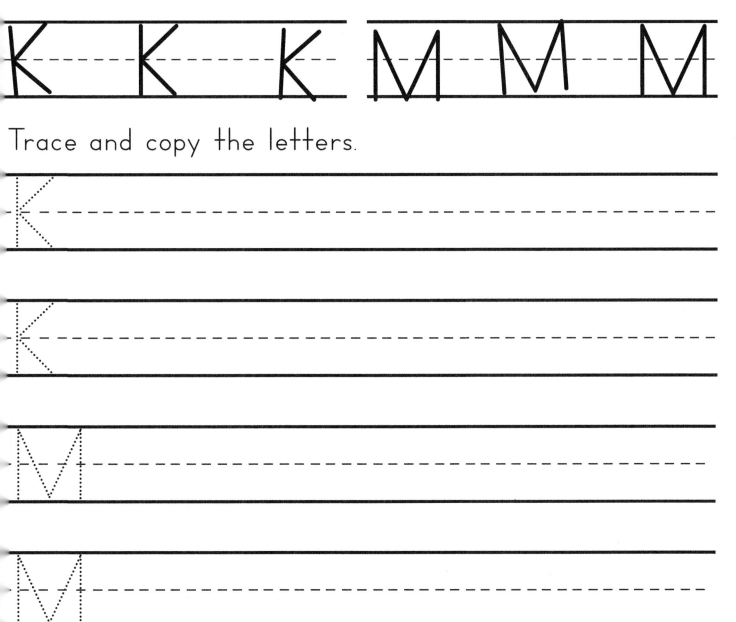

K   K   K   M   M   M   M

Trace and copy the letters.

Joke Time!

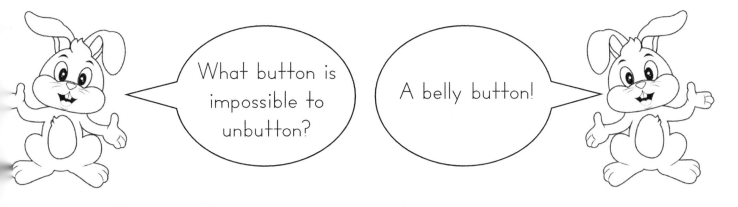

What button is impossible to unbutton?

A belly button!

This is the letter N on handwriting lines.

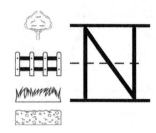

Circle the correct answers below.

N is a	It stands on the	and is as tall as the
tall letter. short letter. tail letter.	tree line fence line grass line dirt line	trees. fence.

Start with your pencil on the dot and write the letter.

This is the letter V on handwriting lines.

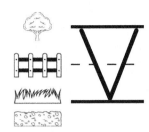

Circle the correct answers below.

V is a	It stands on the	and is as tall as the
tall letter. short letter. tail letter.	tree 🌳 line fence ▦ line grass 〰 line dirt ▦ line	trees. 🌳 fence. ▦

Start with your pencil on the dot and write the letter.

Review

Circle the letters that are in the best positions.

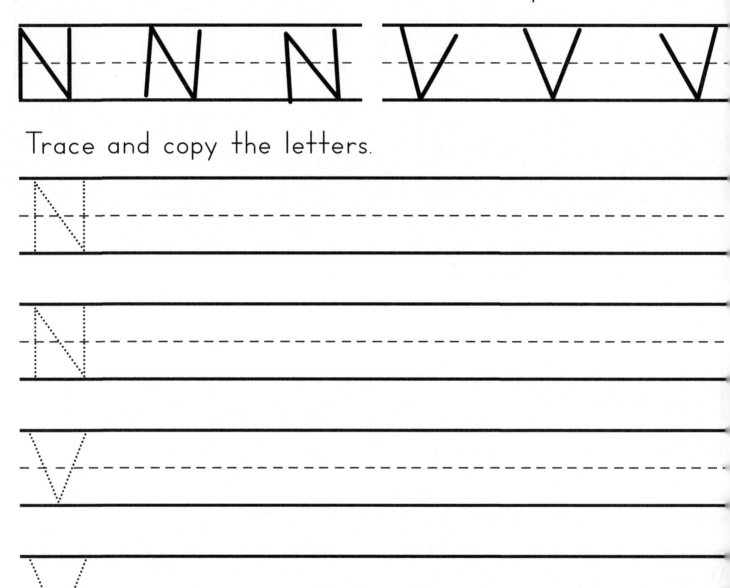

N   N   N   V   V   V

Trace and copy the letters.

Joke Time!

What do you get when you cross a turtle with a porcupine?

A slowpoke!

This is the letter W on handwriting lines.

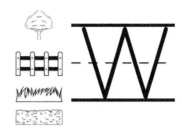

Circle the correct answers below.

W is a	It stands on the	and is as tall as the
tall letter. short letter. tail letter.	tree line fence line grass line dirt line	trees. fence.

Start with your pencil on the dot and write the letter.

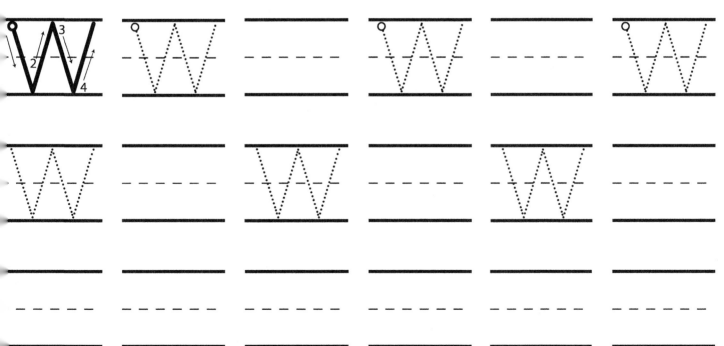

This is the letter X on handwriting lines.

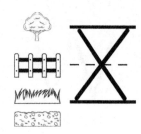

Circle the correct answers below.

X is a	It stands on the	and is as tall as the
tall letter. short letter. tail letter.	tree 🌳 line fence ▦ line grass 〰 line dirt ▨ line	trees. 🌳 fence. ▦

Start with your pencil on the dot and write the letter.

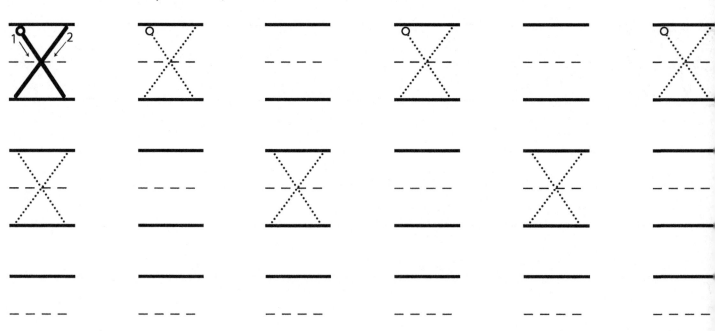

Review

Circle the letters that are in the best positions.

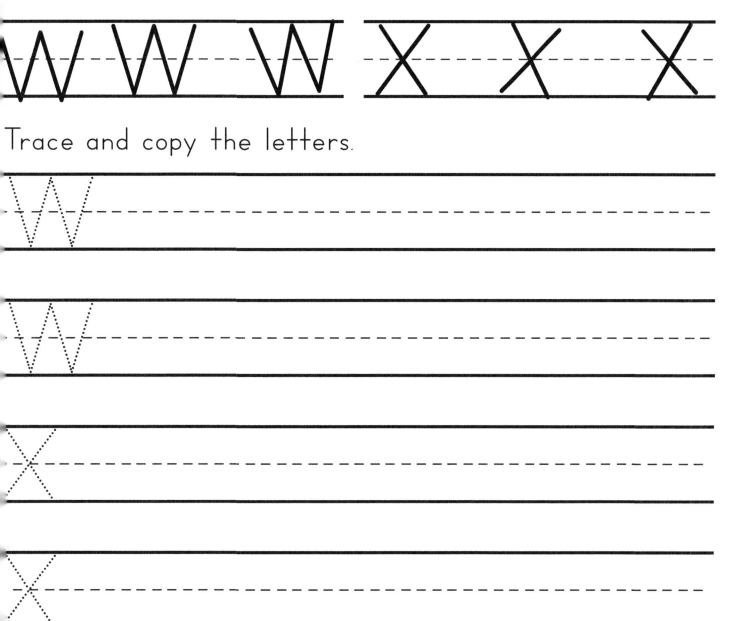

Trace and copy the letters.

Joke Time!

If a seagull flies over the sea, what flies over the bay?

A bagel!

This is the letter Y on handwriting lines.

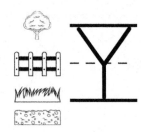

Circle the correct answers below.

Y is a	It stands on the	and is as tall as the
tall letter. short letter. tail letter.	tree 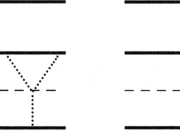 line fence line grass line dirt line	trees. fence. 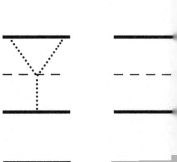

Start with your pencil on the dot and write the letter.

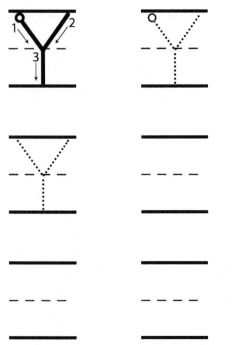

This is the letter Z on handwriting lines.

Circle the correct answers below.

Z is a	It stands on the	and is as tall as the
tall letter. short letter. tail letter.	tree  line fence line grass line dirt line	trees. fence.

Start with your pencil on the dot and write the letter.

Review

Circle the letters that are in the best positions.

Y Y Y Y   Z Z Z Z

Trace and copy the letters.

Y

Y

Z

Z

Joke Time!

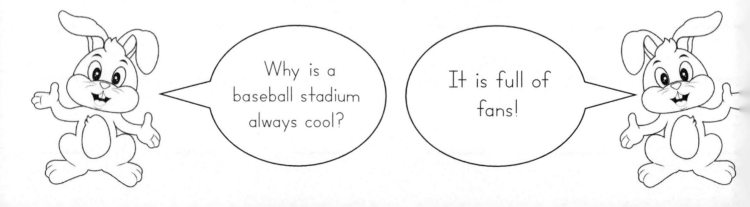

Why is a baseball stadium always cool?

It is full of fans!

This is the number 1 on handwriting lines.

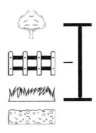

Circle the correct answers below.

1 is a	It stands on the	and is as tall as the
tall number. short number. tail number.	tree  line fence 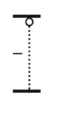 line grass line dirt line	trees. fence.

Start with your pencil on the dot and write the number.

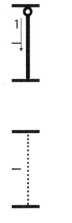 

This is the number 4 on handwriting lines.

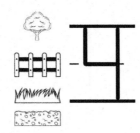

Circle the correct answers below.

4 is a	It stands on the	and is as tall as the
tall number. short number. tail number.	tree line fence line grass line dirt line	trees. fence.

Start with your pencil on the dot and write the number.

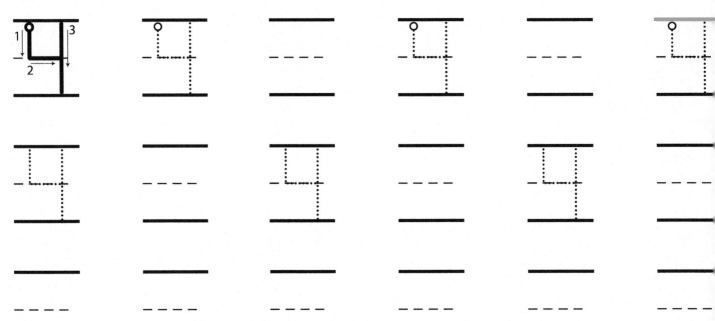

Review

Circle the numbers that are in the best positions.

1   1   1   4   4   4

Trace and copy the numbers.

Joke Time!

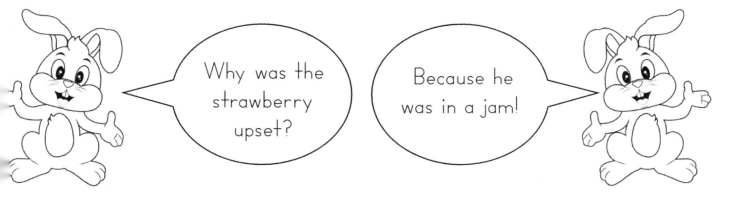

Why was the strawberry upset?

Because he was in a jam!

This is the number 5 on handwriting lines.

Circle the correct answers below.

5 is a	It stands on the	and is as tall as the
tall number. short number. tail number.	tree 🌳 line fence ▦ line grass 〰 line dirt ▦ line	 trees. 🌳 fence. ▦

Start with your pencil on the dot and write the number.

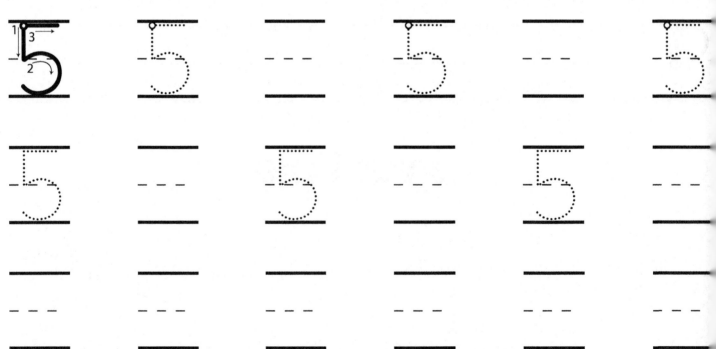

This is the number 9 on handwriting lines.

Circle the correct answers below.

9 is a	It stands on the	and is as tall as the
tall number. short number. tail number.	tree line fence line grass line dirt line	trees. fence.

Start with your pencil on the dot and write the number.

Review

Circle the numbers that are in the best positions.

5   5   5   9   9   9

Trace and copy the numbers.

5

5

9

9

Joke Time!

What's the difference between a guitar and a fish?

You can tune a guitar, but you can't tuna fish!

This is the number 0 on handwriting lines.

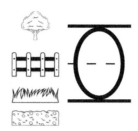

Circle the correct answers below.

0 is a	It stands on the	and is as tall as the
tall number.	tree line	
short number.	fence line	trees.
tail number.	grass line	fence.
	dirt line	

Start with your pencil on the dot and write the number.

This is the number 6 on handwriting lines.

Circle the correct answers below.

6 is a	It stands on the	and is as tall as the
tall number.	tree 🌳 line	
short number.	fence ▦ line	trees. 🌳
tail number.	grass 〰 line	fence. ▦
	dirt ▨ line	

Start with your pencil on the dot and write the number.

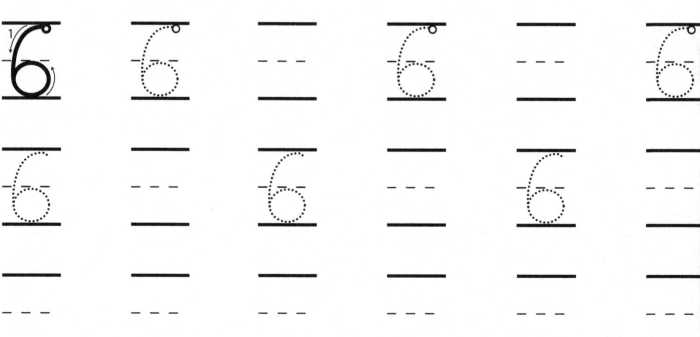

Review

Circle the numbers that are in the best positions.

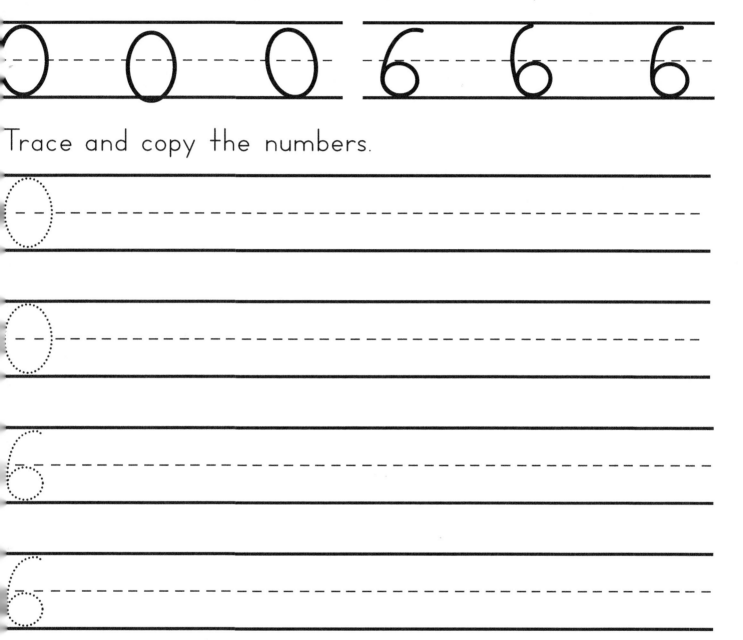

0   0   0   6   6   6

Trace and copy the numbers.

Joke Time!

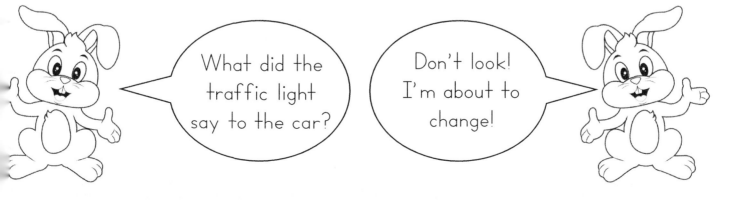

What did the traffic light say to the car?

Don't look! I'm about to change!

This is the number 3 on handwriting lines.

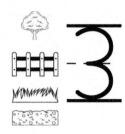

Circle the correct answers below.

3 is a	It stands on the	and is as tall as the
tall number. short number. tail number.	tree line fence line grass line dirt line	trees. fence.

Start with your pencil on the dot and write the number.

This is the number 8 on handwriting lines.

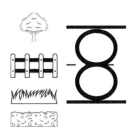

Circle the correct answers below.

8 is a	It stands on the	and is as tall as the
tall number. short number. tall number.	tree line fence line grass line dirt line	trees. fence.

Start with your pencil on the dot and write the number.

Review

Circle the numbers that are in the best positions.

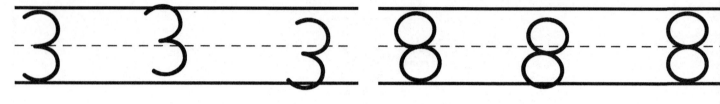

3   3   3   8   8   8

Trace and copy the numbers.

3

3

8

8

Joke Time!

What do you call a fake noodle?

An impasta!

This is the number 2 on handwriting lines.

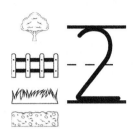

Circle the correct answers below.

2 is a	It stands on the	and is as tall as the
tall number. short number. tail number.	tree  line fence 🠂 line grass  line dirt line	trees. fence. 🠂

Start with your pencil on the dot and write the number.

This is the number 7 on handwriting lines.

Circle the correct answers below.

7 is a	It stands on the	and is as tall as the
tall number. short number. tail number.	tree  line fence line grass line dirt line	trees. fence.

Start with your pencil on the dot and write the number

Review

Circle the numbers that are in the best positions.

2   2   2   7   7   7

Trace and copy the numbers.

2

2

7

7

Joke Time!

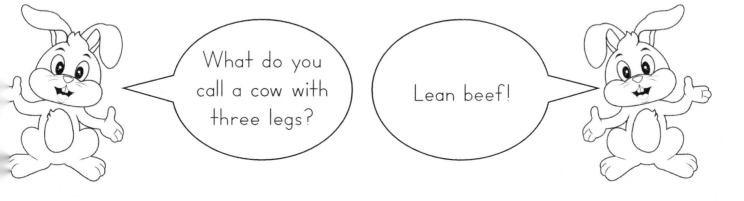

What do you call a cow with three legs?

Lean beef!

Review

Trace and copy the letters.

L   L   - - -   - - -

E   E   - - -   - - -

I   I   - -   - -

D   D   - - -   - - -

P   P   - - -   - - -

U   U   - - -   - - -

F   F   - - -   - - -

H   H   - - -   - - -

I   I   - -   - -

B   B   - - -   - - -

J   J   - - -   - - -

C   C   - - -   - - -

Review

Trace and copy the letters.

O

G

Q

S

R

A

K

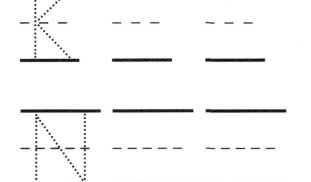

M

N

V

W

X

Review

Trace and copy the letters and numbers.

Y

I

5

0

3

2

Z

4

9

6

8

7

This is the letter l on handwriting lines.

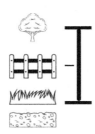

Circle the correct answers below.

l is a	It stands on the	and is as tall as the
tall letter. short letter. tail letter.	tree line fence line grass line dirt line	trees. fence.

Start with your pencil on the dot and write the letter.

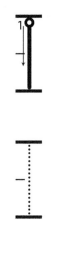  

This is the letter t on handwriting lines.

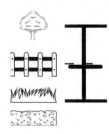

Circle the correct answers below.

t is a	It stands on the	and is as tall as the
tall letter. short letter. tail letter.	tree ⬆ line fence ⊞ line grass ⬆ line dirt ⬆ line	trees. 🌳 fence. ⊞

Start with your pencil on the dot and write the letter.

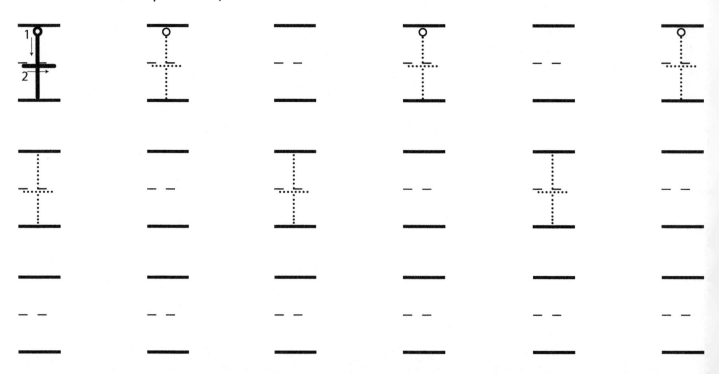

This is the letter i on handwriting lines.

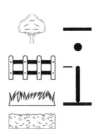

Circle the correct answers below.

i is a	It stands on the	and is as tall as the
tall letter. short letter. tail letter.	tree line fence line grass line dirt line	trees. fence.

Start with your pencil on the dot and write the letter.

Review

Circle the letters that are in the best positions.

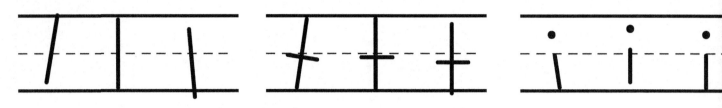

Trace and copy the letters.

Joke Time!

How do you get an astronaut's baby to stop crying?

You rocket!

This is the letter s on handwriting lines.

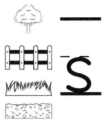

Circle the correct answers below.

s is a	It stands on the	and is as tall as the
tall letter. short letter. tail letter.	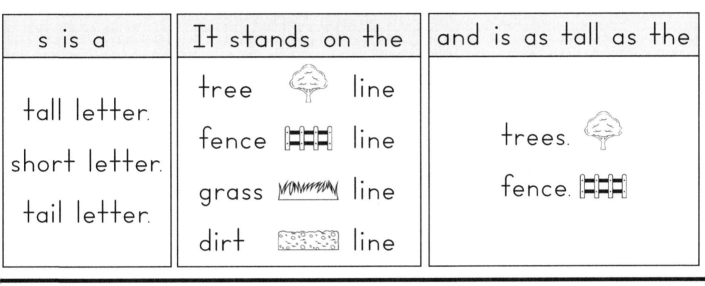tree 🌳 line fence 🚧 line grass 〰 line dirt ▱ line	trees. 🌳 fence. 🚧

Start with your pencil on the dot and write the letter.

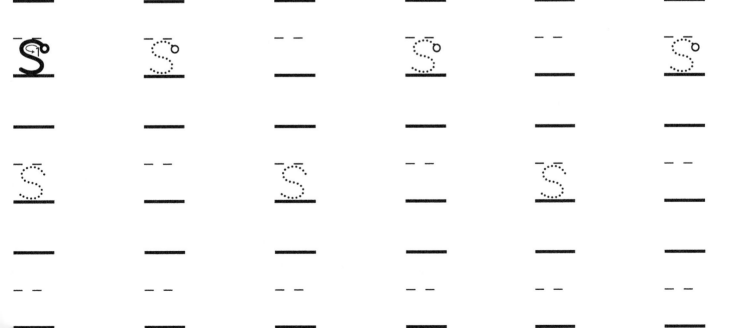

This is the letter c on handwriting lines.

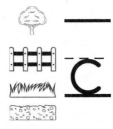

Circle the correct answers below.

c is a	It stands on the	and is as tall as the
tall letter. short letter. tail letter.	tree line fence line grass line dirt line	trees. fence.

Start with your pencil on the dot and write the letter.

This is the letter o on handwriting lines.

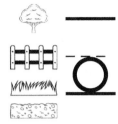

Circle the correct answers below.

o is a	It stands on the	and is as tall as the
tall letter. short letter. tail letter.	tree line fence ▦ line grass 〰 line dirt ▦ line	trees.  fence.

Start with your pencil on the dot and write the letter.

Review

Circle the letters that are in the best positions.

s s s   c c c   o o o

Trace and copy the letters.

s

c

o

s   c   o

Joke Time!

What did the paper say to the pencil?

Write on!

This is the letter a on handwriting lines.

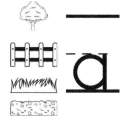

Circle the correct answers below.

a is a	It stands on the	and is as tall as the
tall letter. short letter. tail letter.	tree line fence line grass line dirt line	trees. fence.

Start with your pencil on the dot and write the letter.

This is the letter d on handwriting lines.

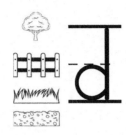

Circle the correct answers below.

d is a	It stands on the	and is as tall as the
tall letter. short letter. tail letter.	tree 🌳 line fence ▦ line grass 🌿 line dirt ▨ line	trees. 🌳 fence. ▦

Start with your pencil on the dot and write the letter.

Review

Circle the letters that are in the best positions.

a a a d d d

Trace and copy the letters.

a

a

a

a

Joke Time!

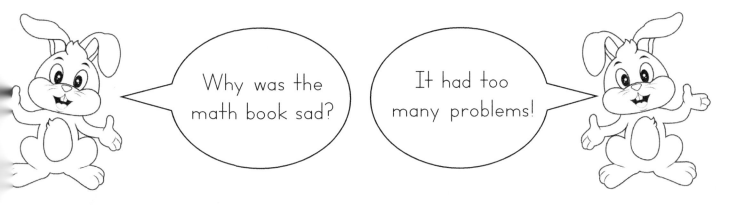

Why was the math book sad?

It had too many problems!

This is the letter g on handwriting lines.

Circle the correct answers below.

g is a	It stands on the	and is as tall as the
tall letter. short letter. tail letter.	tree 🌳 line fence ▦ line grass 🌿 line dirt ▨ line	trees. 🌳 fence. ▦

Start with your pencil on the dot and write the letter.

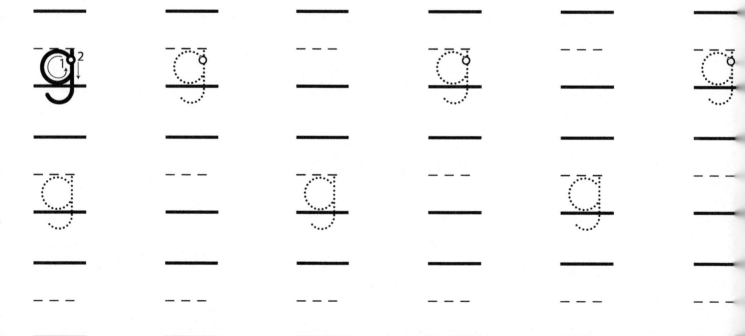

This is the letter q on handwriting lines.

Circle the correct answers below.

q is a	It stands on the	and is as tall as the
tall letter. short letter. tail letter.	tree 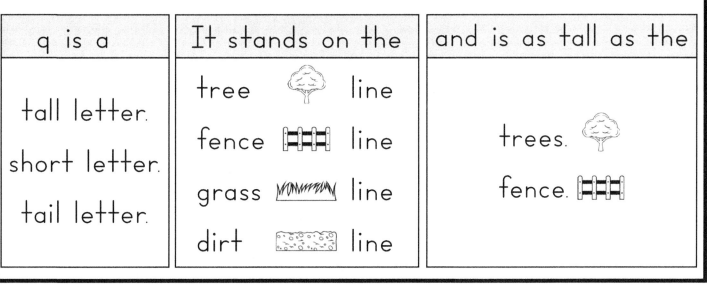 line fence line grass line dirt line	trees. fence.

Start with your pencil on the dot and write the letter.

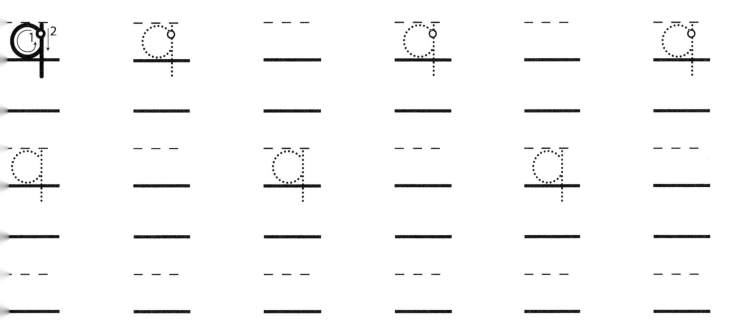

Review

Circle the letters that are in the best positions.

g   g   g   q   q   q

Trace and copy the letters.

g

g

q

q

Joke Time!

What can you catch, but never throw?

A cold!

Trace and Copy

Trace and copy each word once.

sad

dad

gas

sit

cod

rod

cold

Trace and Copy

Trace and copy each word once.

still

sold

dogs

cots

gold

glad

good

This is the letter u on handwriting lines.

Circle the correct answers below.

u is a	It stands on the	and is as tall as the
tall letter. short letter. tail letter.	tree 🌳 line fence ▦ line grass 🌿 line dirt ▦ line	trees. 🌳 fence. ▦

Start with your pencil on the dot and write the letter.

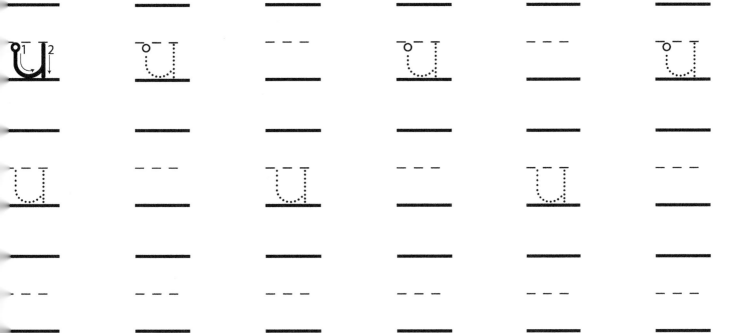

This is the letter j on handwriting lines.

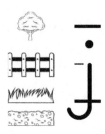

Circle the correct answers below.

j is a	It stands on the	and is as tall as the
tall letter. short letter. tail letter.	tree 🌳 line fence ▦ line grass 🌾 line dirt ▦ line	trees. 🌳 fence. ▦

Start with your pencil on the dot and write the letter.

Review

Circle the letters that are in the best positions.

u   u   u   j   j   j

Trace and copy the letters.

u

u

j

j

Joke Time!

Why did the golfer wear two pairs of socks?

In case he got a hole in one!

This is the letter h on handwriting lines.

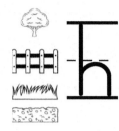

Circle the correct answers below.

h is a	It stands on the	and is as tall as the
tall letter. short letter. tail letter.	tree line fence 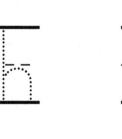 line grass  line dirt  line	trees.  fence. 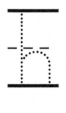

Start with your pencil on the dot and write the letter.

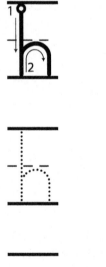

This is the letter n on handwriting lines.

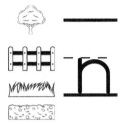

Circle the correct answers below.

n is a	It stands on the	and is as tall as the
tall letter.	tree line	
short letter.	fence line	trees.
tail letter.	grass line	fence.
	dirt line	

Start with your pencil on the dot and write the letter.

Review

Circle the letters that are in the best positions.

h   h   h   n   n   n

Trace and copy the letters.

Trace and copy the letters.

Joke Time!

Why is dark spelled with a K and not a C?

Because you can't see in the dark!

This is the letter m on handwriting lines.

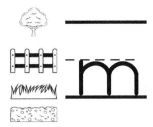

Circle the correct answers below.

m is a	It stands on the	and is as tall as the
tall letter. short letter. tail letter.	tree line fence line grass line dirt line	trees. fence.

Start with your pencil on the dot and write the letter.

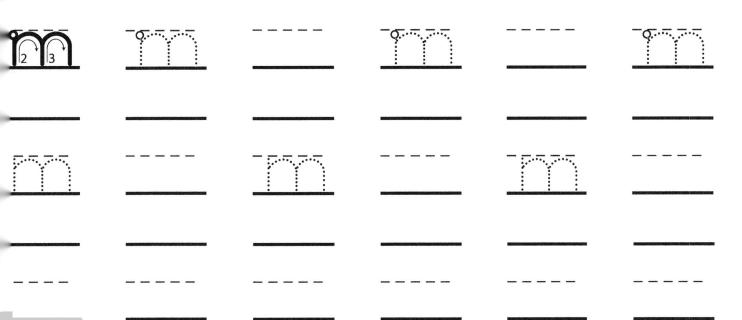

This is the letter r on handwriting lines.

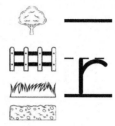

Circle the correct answers below.

r is a	It stands on the	and is as tall as the
tall letter. short letter. tail letter.	tree 🌳 line fence ▦ line grass 〰 line dirt ▦ line	trees. 🌳 fence. ▦

Start with your pencil on the dot and write the letter

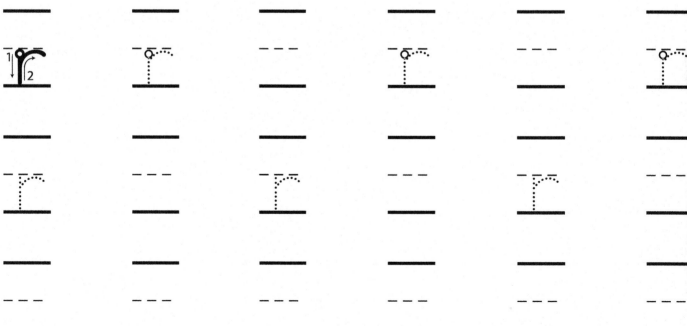

Review

Circle the letters that are in the best positions.

m   m   m   r   r   r

Trace and copy the letters.

m

m

r

r

Joke Time!

What did the stamp say to the envelope?

Stick with me, and we'll go places!

This is the letter b on handwriting lines.

Circle the correct answers below.

b is a	It stands on the	and is as tall as the
tall letter. short letter. tail letter.	tree line fence line grass line dirt line	trees. fence.

Start with your pencil on the dot and write the letter.

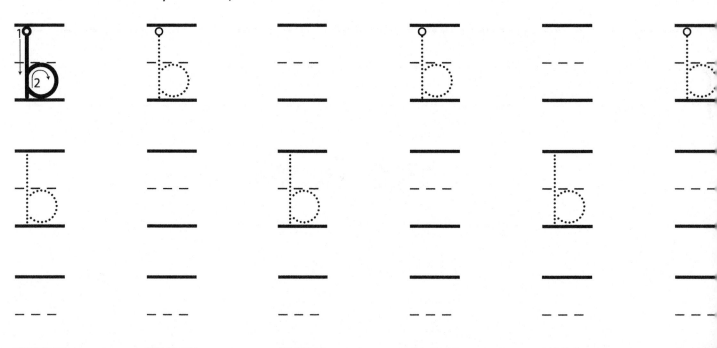

This is the letter p on handwriting lines.

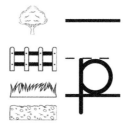

Circle the correct answers below.

p is a	It stands on the	and is as tall as the
tall letter. short letter. tail letter.	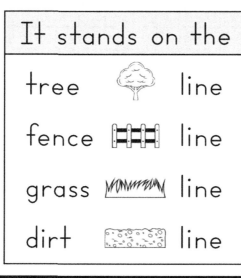 tree line fence line grass line dirt line	 trees. fence.

Start with your pencil on the dot and write the letter.

Review

Circle the letters that are in the best positions.

b   b   b   p   p   p   p

Trace and copy the letters.

b

b

p

p

Joke Time!

Why did the man run around his bed?

To catch up on his sleep!

Trace and Copy

Trace and copy each word once.

up

run

had

big

hut

bun

him

Trace and Copy

Trace and copy each word once.

man

hat

jar

quit

bump

quit

jump

This is the letter v on handwriting lines.

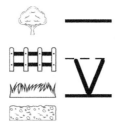

Circle the correct answers below.

v is a	It stands on the	and is as tall as the
tall letter.	tree 🌳 line	
short letter.	fence ▦ line	trees. 🌳
tail letter.	grass ⋀⋀ line	fence. ▦
	dirt ⋯ line	

Start with your pencil on the dot and write the letter.

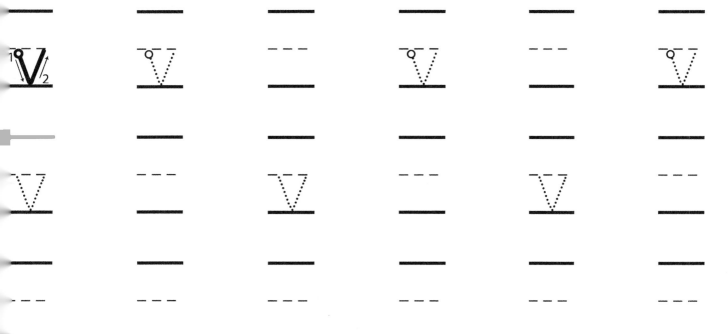

This is the letter w on handwriting lines.

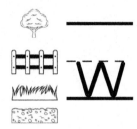

Circle the correct answers below.

w is a	It stands on the	and is as tall as the
tall letter. short letter. tail letter.	tree line fence line grass line dirt line	trees. fence.

Start with your pencil on the dot and write the letter

w   w   w   w

w   w   w

Review

Circle the letters that are in the best positions.

V   V   V   V   W   W   W   W

Trace and copy the letters.

V

V

W

W

Joke Time!

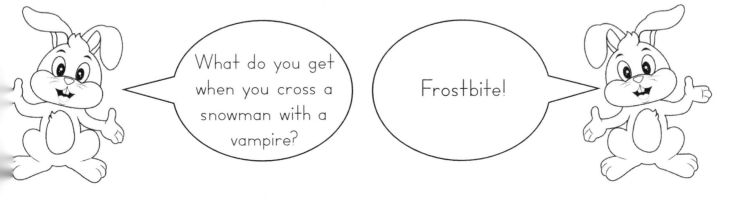

What do you get when you cross a snowman with a vampire?

Frostbite!

This is the letter x on handwriting lines.

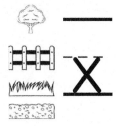

Circle the correct answers below.

x is a	It stands on the	and is as tall as the
tall letter. short letter. tail letter.	tree 🌳 line fence ▦ line grass 🌾 line dirt ▨ line	trees. 🌳 fence. ▦

Start with your pencil on the dot and write the letter.

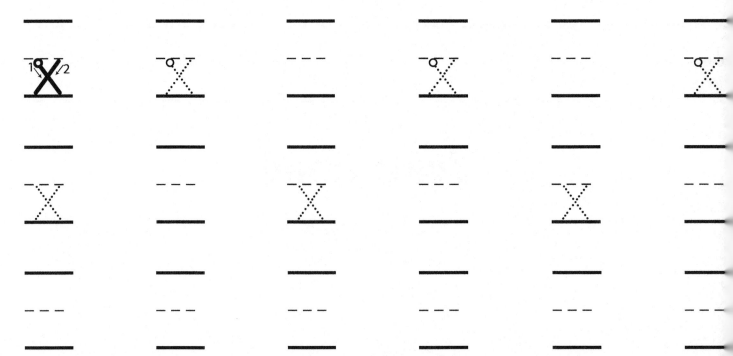

Need help forming z? See our YouTube video, How to Write the Lowercase Letter z

Lesson z

This is the letter z on handwriting lines.

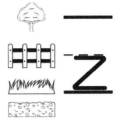

Circle the correct answers below.

z is a	It stands on the	and is as tall as the
tall letter. short letter. tail letter.	tree line fence line grass line dirt line	trees. fence.

Start with your pencil on the dot and write the letter.

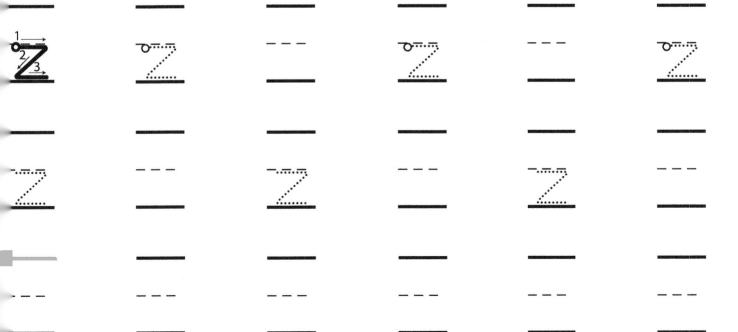

Review

Circle the letters that are in the best positions.

X   X   X   Z   Z   Z

Trace and copy the letters.

x

x

z

z

Joke Time!

Where do roses sleep at night?

In their flowerbeds!

This is the letter k on handwriting lines.

Circle the correct answers below.

k is a	It stands on the	and is as tall as the
tall letter. short letter. tail letter.	tree 🌳 line fence ▦ line grass 🌾 line dirt ▦ line	trees. 🌳 fence. ▦

Start with your pencil on the dot and write the letter.

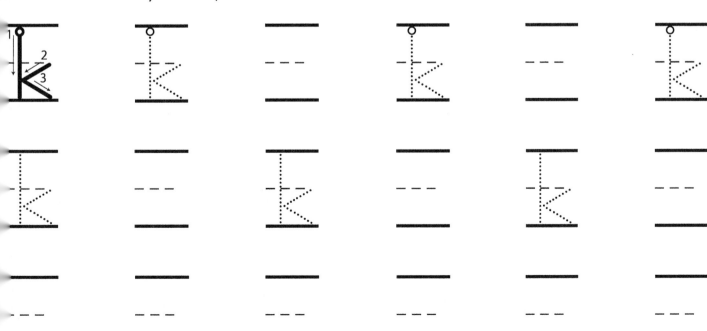

This is the letter y on handwriting lines.

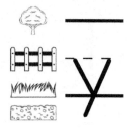

Circle the correct answers below.

y is a	It stands on the	and is as tall as the
tall letter. short letter. tail letter.	tree ☁ line fence ‖‖ line grass 〰 line dirt ▦ line	trees. 🌳 fence. ‖‖

Start with your pencil on the dot and write the letter.

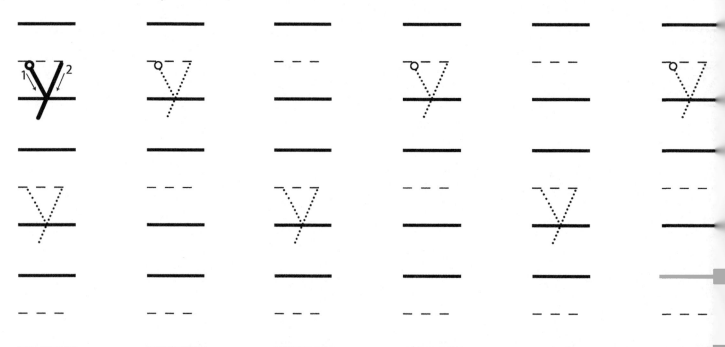

Review

Circle the letters that are in the best positions.

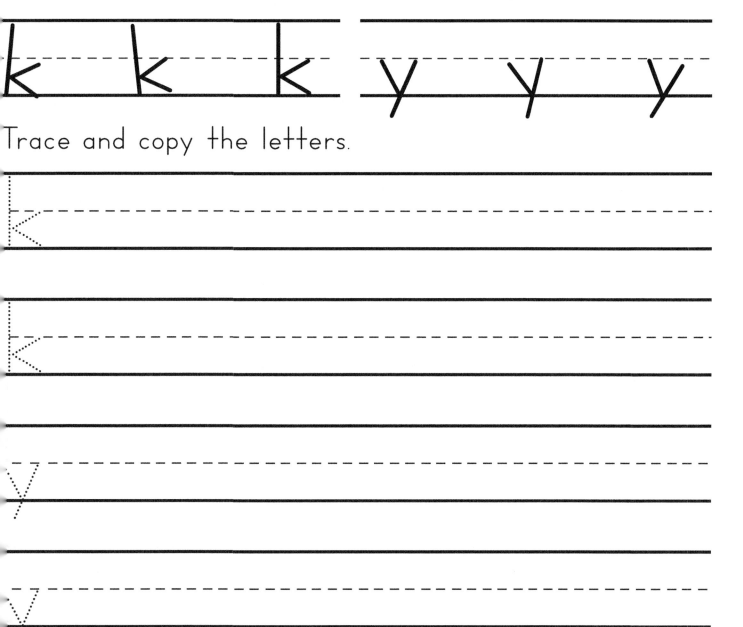

k   k   k   y   y   y

Trace and copy the letters.

Joke Time!

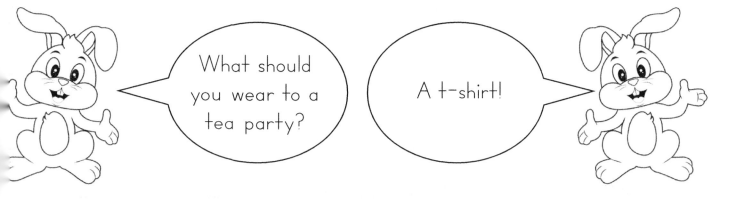

What should you wear to a tea party?

A t-shirt!

This is the letter e on handwriting lines.

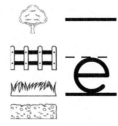

Circle the correct answers below.

e is a	It stands on the	and is as tall as the
tall letter. short letter. tail letter.	tree 🌳 line fence ▦ line grass 〰 line dirt ▒ line	trees. 🌳 fence. ▦

Start with your pencil on the dot and write the letter.

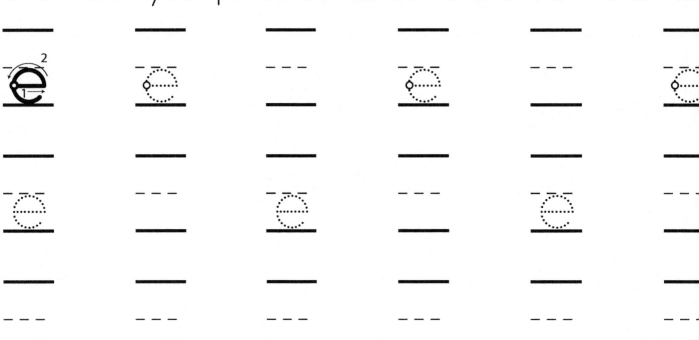

This is the letter f on handwriting lines.

Circle the correct answers below.

f is a	It stands on the	and is as tall as the
tall letter. short letter. tail letter.	tree line fence line grass line dirt line	 trees. fence.

Start with your pencil on the dot and write the letter.

Review

Circle the letters that are in the best positions.

e   e   e   f   f   f

Trace and copy the letters.

e

e

f

f

Joke Time!

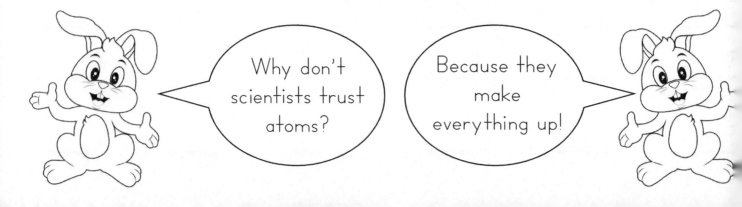

Why don't scientists trust atoms?

Because they make everything up!

Trace and Copy

Trace and copy each word once.

key

zip

was

fox

for

box

fox

Trace and Copy

Trace and copy each word once.

kid

fall

well

vote

went

fuzz

have

Review

Trace and copy the letters.

I   I   i

s   c   o

a   d

g   q

u   j

h   n

Review

Trace and copy the letters.

m   r

b   p

v   w

x   z

k   y

e   f

Self Assessment

Hi friends! I'm so proud of you for completing this workbook! The last thing that I want you to do is complete this self-assessment. First, copy the letter or number. Then, circle the face that describes how you feel about writing the letter. Try not to do more than one page at a time, and you can stop whenever you want. You're doing great!

Self Assessment

A	☺ ☺ ☹	B	☺ ☺ ☹
C	☺ ☺ ☹	D	☺ ☺ ☹
E	☺ ☺ ☹	F	☺ ☺ ☹
G	☺ ☺ ☹	H	☺ ☺ ☹
I	☺ ☺ ☹	J	☺ ☺ ☹
K	☺ ☺ ☹	L	☺ ☺ ☹
M	☺ ☺ ☹	N	☺ ☺ ☹

Self Assessment

O	☺ ☺ ☹	P	☺ ☺ ☹
Q	☺ ☺ ☹	R	☺ ☺ ☹
S	☺ ☺ ☹	T	☺ ☺ ☹
U	☺ ☺ ☹	V	☺ ☺ ☹
W	☺ ☺ ☹	X	☺ ☺ ☹
Y	☺ ☺ ☹	Z	☺ ☺ ☹

Self Assessment

a		☺ ☺ ☹	b		☺ ☺ ☹
c		☺ ☺ ☹	d		☺ ☺ ☹
e		☺ ☺ ☹	f		☺ ☺ ☹
g		☺ ☺ ☹	h		☺ ☺ ☹
i		☺ ☺ ☹	j		☺ ☺ ☹
k		☺ ☺ ☹	l		☺ ☺ ☹
m		☺ ☺ ☹	n		☺ ☺ ☹

Self Assessment

o		☺ ☺ ☹	p		☺ ☺ ☹
q		☺ ☺ ☹	r		☺ ☺ ☹
s		☺ ☺ ☹	t		☺ ☺ ☹
u		☺ ☺ ☹	v		☺ ☺ ☹
w		☺ ☺ ☹	x		☺ ☺ ☹
y		☺ ☺ ☹	z		☺ ☺ ☹

Self Assessment

0		☺ ☺ ☹	1		☺ ☺ ☹
2		☺ ☺ ☹	3		☺ ☺ ☹
4		☺ ☺ ☹	5		☺ ☺ ☹
6		☺ ☺ ☹	7		☺ ☺ ☹
8		☺ ☺ ☹	9		☺ ☺ ☹

Certificate

Congratulations! You've finished Handwriting Practice Made Fun: Focus on Size and Placement! You did a great job. Visit our website for a downloadable certificate to celebrate your achievement. I can't wait to see you in the next workbook.

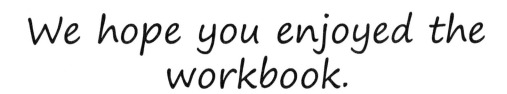

We hope you enjoyed the workbook.

Please leave us a review.

Printed in Great Britain
by Amazon

45223551R00071